Go Outside!
GO FOR A
SWIM!

By Peter Finn

Gareth Stevens
PUBLISHING

Please visit our website, www.garethstevens.com. For a free color catalog of all our high-quality books, call toll free 1-800-542-2595 or fax 1-877-542-2596.

Library of Congress Cataloging-in-Publication Data

Names: Finn, Peter, 1978- author.
Title: Go for a swim! / Peter Finn.
Description: New York : Gareth Stevens Publishing, [2020] | Series: Go outside! | Includes index.
Identifiers: LCCN 2019010251| ISBN 9781538244890 (pbk.) | ISBN 9781538244913 (library bound) | ISBN 9781538244906 (6 pack)
Subjects: LCSH: Swimming–Juvenile literature.
Classification: LCC GV837.6 .F53 2020 | DDC 797.2/1–dc23
LC record available at https://lccn.loc.gov/2019010251

Published in 2020 by
Gareth Stevens Publishing
111 East 14th Street, Suite 349
New York, NY 10003

Editor: Therese Shea
Designer: Sarah Liddell

Photo credits: Cover, p. 1 Lopolo/Shutterstock.com; pp. 5, 23 YanLev/Shutterstock.com; p. 7 pio3/Shutterstock.com; p. 9 BlueOrange/Shutterstock.com; p. 11 Golden Pixels LLC/Shutterstock.com; pp. 13, 24 (diving board) Jon Feingersh/The Image Bank/Getty Images Plus/Getty Images; p. 15 altanaka/Shutterstock.com; p. 17 BRG.photography/Shutterstock.com; pp. 19, 24 (butterfly) Suzanne Tucker/Shutterstock.com; p. 21 Suwan Wanawattanawong/Shutterstock.com.

Printed in the United States of America

Some of the images in this book illustrate individuals who are models. The depictions do not imply actual situations or events.

CPSIA compliance information: Batch #CW20GS: For further information contact Gareth Stevens, New York, New York at 1-800-542-2595.

Contents

Meet Ava. 4

Where We Swim 6

Having Fun 12

On the Team 16

Go Swimming!. 22

Words to Know 24

Index. 24

My name is Ava.
I love to swim!

We swim many places.
We swim in the lake.

We swim in
the ocean.

We swim at the pool.

Dev jumps off
the diving board!

13

We play games
in the water.
Marco Polo is like
hide-and-seek!

This is my swim team.
We race in the water.

I swim the butterfly.
It's a special stroke.

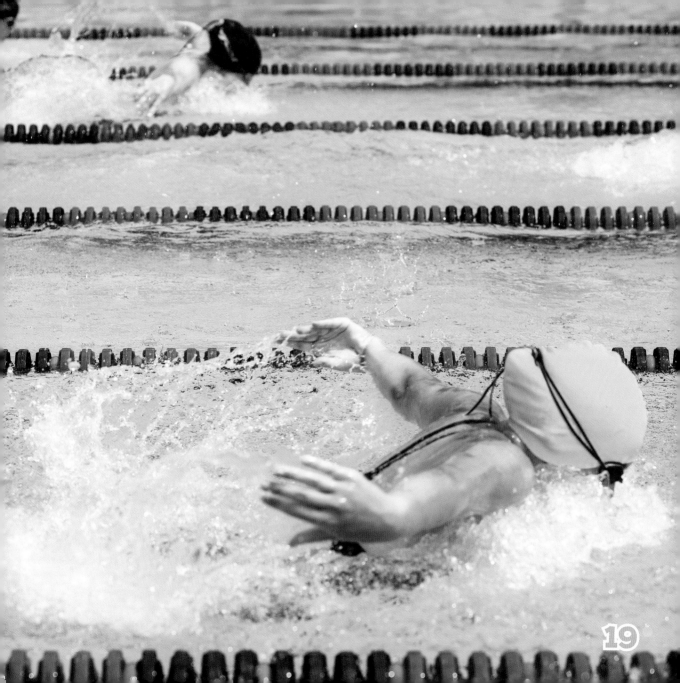

I practice to get faster.
I win first place!

Swimming is good exercise. Go swimming!

Words to Know

butterfly

diving board

Index

butterfly 18

diving board 12

exercise 22

Marco Polo 14

stroke 18

team 16